NATIONAL MONUMENTS RECORD · PHOTOGRAPHIC ARCHIVES

Yesterday's Gardens

Alastair Forsyth

GENERAL EDITOR

Peter Fowler

ROYAL COMMISSION ON HISTORICAL MONUMENTS ENGLAND

LONDON HER MAJESTY'S STATIONERY OFFICE

© Crown copyright 1983
First published 1983

ISBN 0 11 701126 6

HER MAJESTY'S STATIONERY OFFICE

Government Bookshops

49 High Holborn, London WC1V 6HB
13a Castle Street, Edinburgh EH2 3AR
Brazennose Street, Manchester M60 8AS
Southey House, Wine Street, Bristol BS1 2BQ
258 Broad Street, Birmingham B1 2HE
80 Chichester Street, Belfast BT1 4JY

Government publications are also available
through booksellers

SELECT BIBLIOGRAPHY

J. Anthony, *Discovering Period Gardens*. Shire Publications. 1972
Marcus Binney and Anne Hills, *Elysian Gardens*. Save Britain's Heritage. 1979
Gertrude Jekyll, *Garden Ornament*. Country Life. 1918
Thomas Mawson, *The Art and Craft of Garden Making*. B.T. Batsford. 1900, 1926
G. Taylor, *The Victorian Flower Garden*. Skeffington. 1952
Grahame Stuart Thomas, *Gardens of the National Trust*. Weidenfeld and Nicolson. 1979
H. Avray Tipping, *English Gardens*. Country Life. 1925
Mrs Harriet Osgood Taylour, *Japanese Gardens*. Methuen. 1928

Printed in England for Her Majesty's Stationery Office
by Jolly & Barber Ltd, Rugby

Dd 717084 C50

EDITOR'S FOREWORD

All the photographs in this book are held in the National Monuments Record (NMR), a national archive which is part of the Royal Commission on Historical Monuments (England). The NMR originated in 1941 as the National Buildings Record which, at a time when so much was being destroyed, took upon itself the task of photographing as many historic buildings as possible before it was too late. The Record continued its work after the War and was transferred to the Royal Commission in 1963. As the NMR, it now covers both architectural and archaeological subjects and contains well over a million photographs, together with maps, plans and other documents, relating to England's man-made heritage. The NMR is a public archive, open from 10.00 – 17.30 hours on weekdays; prints can be supplied to order on payment of the appropriate fee.

This book is the fourth of a series intended to illustrate the wealth of photographic material publicly available in the NMR. Many of the photographs are valuable in their own right, either because of their age or because they are the only records we now possess of buildings, and even whole environments, which have disappeared. Unlike other Commission publications, these are primarily picture-books, drawing entirely on what happens to be in the NMR. No attempt is made to treat each subject comprehensively nor to accompany it with a deeply researched text, but the text and captions are intended to give meaning to the photographs by indicating a context within which they can be viewed. It would be pleasing if they suggested lines of enquiry for others to follow. The titles in the series show where the strengths of the archive lie. Equally, of course, the collection is weak in some respects, and I hope that many of those who see this volume may be reminded of old, and perhaps disregarded, photographs of buildings and scenes in their possession. We would be glad to be told of the whereabouts of such photographs as potential contributions to the national record of our architectural and archaeological heritage.

The selection of photographs published here celebrates some of the most attractive gardens in Victorian and Edwardian England. Some are well-known and some survive, others are less familiar or have disappeared. These photographs allow us to glimpse, in the context of contemporary taste and theory, some of the creations which contributed to what we have come to expect of 'the English garden'. As an interest in garden history develops beside the tremendously popular activity of gardening itself, pictures such as these remind us that a garden in bloom is, at the time, a sort of monument to its age but yet one step away from becoming, through neglect, a more conventional archaeological monument of grass-covered terraces and mounds.

Royal Commission on Historical
Monuments (England),
Fortress House,
23 Savile Row,
London W1X 1AB

Peter Fowler,
Secretary,
Royal Commission on
Historical Monuments (England);
General Editor,
NMR Photographic Archives

ACKNOWLEDGEMENTS

The Commission is grateful for permission to reproduce photographs in the National Monuments Record of which the copyright is held by:

Maj.-Gen. Sir Allan Adair, Bt.
Sir John Cotterell, Bt.
C.R. Fraser-Jenkins
M.J. Marson
Oxfordshire County Libraries
Royal Institute of British Architects
G.C. Royle
Major D. Hill-Wood

The author thanks many individuals and institutions for their help, in particular: Miss Rosemary Angel (Officer in Charge, Museums Division, Royal Botanic Gardens, Kew), Mrs. J. Balcon, Lady Diana Cooper, Mr. M. Diebel, Miss Valerie Forsyth, Major-General Graham (Chevening Estate Office), Mr R. Harcourt Williams (Hatfield House), Mrs Marion Hinton (Heritage Officer, Kingston upon Thames), Miss M. Holmes (Dorset County Record Office), Mr Hyde (Headmaster, Swaylands School), Mr P.M. Reid, Mr Rigby (Newbold College), Miss Naomi Rugg-Gunn, Mrs Marianne Thorn (Swaylands Study Centre), Mr G.M. Warren (HMSO).

The author also thanks colleagues on the Commission staff, especially Miss P. Ashley-Evans, Dr J. Bold, Mr R. Flanders, Mrs D. Kendall and staff in the Order Section, and Mr R. Parsons and staff in the Photographic section.

(*front cover*) The Platt, Hestercombe House, Somerset. NMR, 1982.
(*frontispiece*) Old garden wall, Hatfield House, Hertfordshire. W.J. Day, *c*.1907.
(*inside back endpaper*) Terracotta group, Holland House, Kensington and Chelsea, London. W.J. Day, *c*.1907.

Gardeners at Hestercombe House, Somerset in 1914.
NMR, 1982. Copyright Somerset County Council.

Yesterday's Gardens

INTRODUCTION

Most of the pictures in this book show gardens created during the reigns of Queen Victoria and King Edward VII. The scale on which many of these gardens were created was often grand and luxurious; clearly many owners were uninhibited by financial considerations. Mass labour was comparatively cheap and readily, even gratefully available. The efforts of the gardening staff ensured an immaculate appearance, even an air of permanence; yet the garden is transient by nature, and many of the examples shown in this collection have now disappeared. Nevertheless, in a sense these early photographs triumph over the ephemeral nature of the garden and its swift cycle of change. There are no scents or textures here, and the third dimension is only an illusion; but at least the camera has 'captured the moment' thus presenting something of the garden's quality, even though lacking colour. With all its limitations, the photograph gives us a better record than is available from earlier centuries to work from in studying gardens and those who planned, cared and paid for them. The following selection of photographs illustrates some of the developments and variations in English garden design as actually practised from the mid-19th to the early 20th century.

Gardens differed widely in their form and content during these decades; a single 'English' or 'Victorian' type of garden did not predominate. By the end of the 1830s practically every garden style known today had already been thought of in some form. The choice was confusing for the would-be gardener wanting to do the proper thing; eminent gardeners, architects and art critics each urged the merits of their particular, favourite schemes. Uniting the disunity, however, was a widespread interest in the design of gardens, a realization that gardens had to be 'made to happen', that to create a satisfactory garden involved more than just choosing the plants, shrubs and trees to adorn it. Time, too, appeared to be on the gardener's side: the Victorian decades of apparently endless peace encouraged the owners of the many new houses and gardens to think in the long-term, to be ambitious and to express their upper- or middle-class aspirations in a professionally planned garden. To master Nature by creating contemporary order out of old gardens, or from the wild, appealed as much to aristocrats of artistic bent as to thrustingly prosperous *nouveaux-riches*.

The lady of the house played an increasing part in the direction of the garden. In 1840 Jane Loudon wrote in her *Gardening for Ladies* that, respecting the management of the flower garden, 'This is pre-eminently a woman's department'. The choice of plants was often in the hands of women but current garden fashion (a strong factor in personal choice) was largely ordained by men. Gardens, it was sensed, should be tastefully formed; they should attempt to accord with a recognizable style even if, in practice, the result was not always a realization of the patterns in books.

John Claudius Loudon was one of the most influential of garden theorists in mid-Victorian society. He distinguished four basic varieties of garden and suggested various ways in which the necessary artifices could be contrived. The four varieties were the Rustic, imitating the humble cottage garden in a self-conscious but comfortably rough way; the Picturesque, imitating Nature; the Geometric, with the emphasis on formality; and the Gardenesque, calculated to display the varied arts of the gardener. The Rustic and Picturesque gardens had held sway in the 18th and early 19th centuries, but they, so fashion decreed, were now to be superseded in the ideal garden by the Geometric and the Gardenesque.

The Geometric form was most effectively expressed in the style of the French parterre or the Italianate garden. It was extensively adopted from the mid-19th century. Characterized by the use of terraces, geometric flower beds, sculpture, evergreen planting and topiary, it consciously acknowledged a debt to older and foreign sources. The style became popular in the 19th century following the creation of a novel Italian garden at Wilton some time before 1830; it was further established by the great gardens laid out by Charles Barry and W.A. Nesfield at Trentham from 1833 onwards. The Italianate terraces and parterres of the successful East Garden at Hatfield House (Plate 2) laid out a little later (c.1841) was characterized by complex geometric bedding patterns, box hedging and gravels and coloured earths. It was meant to evoke thoughts of Tudor and Jacobean knot gardens while also forming an harmonious and logical continuation from the genuine Jacobean house alongside.

Mazes had featured in many 17th-century gardens. One had been planted at Chevening c.1820 and, from about 1840, the maze became an increasingly popular garden feature. Hatfield (Plate 2) was one of the first Victorian gardens

to have one; Somerleyton (1846) was another. A conceit that tested the resources but offered a reward, the maze was constrained within a framework of clipped formality and conscious historical imitation. In contrast, the yew trees inside the older vineyard at Hatfield (Plate 1) presented a picture of natural growth allowed to go literally 'over the top'. The survival of this 'natural' essay in the Picturesque and Sublime near the formality of the new parterre garden is typical of the eclecticism which is such a marked, and visually often exciting, characteristic of British gardening.

The waywardness of the yew avenue at Hatfield is in contrast to the pleached avenues at Chiswick (Plate 3), rendered ghostly in the selected photograph by the wintry season and the spectral visages of strategically placed busts. Statuary and sculpture on a large scale in regular arrangements contributed to the aura of the new gardens and served as reminders of gardens seen on the Grand Tour. Stone ornaments could be used to border neat walks between avenues of trees, as at Grimston (Plate 4) and adorn terraces as at Witley (Plate 7), Osborne (Plates 5, 6), or later at Brome Hall (Plate 9) and Hardwick House (Plate 10). Some of the most spectacular adventures in this genre included huge fountains and basins. A most impressive example is at Witley Court (Plate 7), where the major feature was the Perseus fountain, famous for its jet, which rose to a height of 30 metres. Perseus survives but not the jet.

One of the most remarkable aspects of the parterre garden (Plates 5, 11-20) was the scope it gave for displaying flowers and other plants. Throughout most of the 19th century, elaborate geometric beds continued to be popular. They were filled with plants often chosen for their variety and rarity rather than their colour and quantity. Many new species were discovered during the 18th and 19th centuries. Annuals such as petunias or verbenas were not available until the 1840s, while geraniums were being bred in new forms throughout the 19th century.

The classical landscape was not ideally disposed to display these plants, which came to jostle with dahlias (Plate 18) and other 'exotics' in patterns of impeccable geometry. Loudon particularly approved the inclusion of non-native species since they emphasized the artificiality of the 'garden' as now conceived. These new forms of display, made possible by the new glasshouses which could provide vast quantities of 'carpet-bedders', were very extravagant to mount. Beds, too, were often bare for four months at a time, though occasionally evergreens were installed during the winter.

The mid-Victorian garden should not, however, be envisaged as entirely 'carpet-bedded'. Shirley Hibberd, for example, wrote (1856) that 'the bedding system is an embellishment added to the garden – the herbaceous border is a necessary fundamental feature'. A border of traditional hardy plants was a feature of most gardens but was not the focus of popular attention in the mid-19th century; its glories were to be more fully achieved over the years 1870-1920 (Plates 23-7). Against a practical background of the parterre and its carpet-bedding, Hibberd was, however, already anticipating a change in garden fashion. He was more interested in flowers and shrubs for their own sake than primarily as part of a grand design; he favoured a gentler landscape of lawns and shrubs with small beds dispersed at will and separated by easy, meandering walks (Plates 28, 29). The garden he had in mind was less concerned with making a statement than with providing a place for relaxed enjoyment. The Italianate garden at Avon Bank, Warwickshire (Plate 30), reflects this loosening of geometric rigidity.

KELMSCOTT MANOR
Edmund Hort New, 1899.

Although really describing the Gardenesque style, Hibberd was in some respects anticipating William Robinson (1838-1934), who, in aiming to make the Gardenesque style more natural, helped to transform popular taste and create a new garden form. He found the Victorian parterre a gross thing, describing carpet-bedding as 'that mean attempt to rival the tile or wallpaper man'. Robinson advocated the herbaceous border, including shrubs; he sought a freer, fuller and more stable effect than carpet-bedding. In *The English Flower Garden* (1883) he said: 'Instead of the beds being nearly as possible the same throughout the season the aim should be to produce the variety of Nature'. His *The Wild Garden* (1870) extolled the virtues of 'naturalism' and demonstrated an extensive knowledge of the traditional cottage garden (Plate 31). Instead of writing a romantic eulogy on the charms of the simple life of the cottager, Robinson summarized the lessons that could be learnt from cottage gardens and reminded his readers of the forgotten ones that could be relearnt. He argued that to apply this knowledge in modern gardens would be to their aesthetic and practical benefit. Gradually, a new garden style emerged. The frame was one of the plainest geometry; the beds were filled with a mixture of shrubs and well-loved hardy plants. Robinson's ideas were best illustrated in his own garden and in the woodland of his estate at Gravetye Manor in Sussex. The garden at Great Tangley in Surrey (Plate 32) was laid out in much the same spirit.

Robinson's love of the cottage garden was shared by William Morris and John Ruskin. The latter approved its honesty on moral grounds. The simplicity of the style was apparent in the old garden Morris maintained at Kelmscott. Morris recommended dividing up the garden into cubicles by hedges or trellises, an arrangement echoing the influence of the kitchen garden (Plates 33, 34). The appeal of the natural garden did not mean, however, that the carpet-bedding system was banished from English gardens; it continued to flourish, leaving Robinson with plenty of material to rage against in his subsequent writings. He particularly detested 'ribbon' bordering as found, for example, at Garnons (Plate 35) and Claremont (Plate 37). He also loathed 'basket' beds, as at Gunnersbury Park (Plate 36) and Belton House (Plate 15), while his preference for traditional and native flowers would certainly have made him view with distaste, had he seen them, the expensive display of 'exotics' and tropical plants on the terrace of the Rothschilds' Gunnersbury House (Plate 38).

Robinson also believed in planting shrubs and trees in clumps. The mass planting of rhododendrons at, for example, Deepdene (Plate 40), Cragside (Plate 45) and Cobham Hall (Plate 27), was one of the most popular versions of this theme; the extensive planting of laurel remained popular but rather less lovely. Robinson did not like to see too many varieties dotted about. In this his views conflicted with Loudon's. The latter welcomed all the new imported species but advised that they should be planted in isolation from each other (Plates 40, 41, 42) to make it clear that they were specimen trees and shrubs. This system, while not always aesthetically satisfactory, effectively proclaimed the botanical pretentions of the collector while indulging a romantic yearning for the exotic. The garden at Tresco (Plate 44) in the Isles of Scilly is a monument to Victorian species collecting.

The laying-out of the grounds at Cragside, Northumberland (Plate 45), between 1870 and 1883 is an astounding example of Victorian energy and ingenuity. The grounds can be seen perhaps as the culmination of the Victorian appreciation of the beauties of woodland and its undergrowth, of common and rare plants, a taste that had grown throughout the 19th century and particularly after the publication of Robinson's books. Yet the appreciation was not so pure as to exclude additions: the Giant Indian Lilies planted in the wood at Pyrford Court (Plate 46) supposedly introduced a

sensuous foreign note to their sylvan background.

Somewhat independent of the Robinsonian natural and cottage garden style was the school of the 'Old Fashioned' or 'Queen Anne' garden. This style was inspired less by gardeners than by architects, painters and poets; its components were in part chosen as much for their historical associations as for their aesthetic attractions. The revival and development of the Old Fashioned garden (Plates 49, 50, 51, 52, 53) was well under way by 1870 and was popular over the next twenty years; after that it merged with a variety of elements (Plates 47, 48). The emphasis was on gentle formality. Occasionally the effect resembled Robinson's natural garden and, later on, the 'garden prettiness' of book illustrations by such artists as Grasset and Greenaway. Popular elements were standard roses growing out of the lawn (Plate 54), clipped hedges (Plate 53), and old-fashioned flowers mixed with vegetables (Plate 50), recalling once more the rustic but sensible simplicities of the kitchen garden (Plate 33). The garden at Pyrford Court (Plates 53, 54), begun as late as 1906, was partly laid out in a manner directly recalling the Queen Anne garden. Such intimacies were also reminiscent of the smaller Dutch garden. On the other hand, the grander formalities and radial planning of the 17th-century Dutch or French palace park influenced the straight avenues that were planted on some estates like Cornbury Park (Plate 55) or Byram Hall (Plate 56). The avenue at Redleaf (Plate 57) with its conifers, rhododendrons and laurels, however, corresponds more closely to the common idea of Victorian taste.

An important aspect of the Dutch garden was its emphasis on topiary. There was nothing revolutionary about the craft of clipping: a very few ancient topiary gardens like Levens (Plate 58) and Chastleton survived, and sporadic attempts to revive the technique had been made since the 1820s. A most spectacular topiary garden was laid out at Elvaston Castle (Plate 59) between 1830 and 1850. Variations on the theme (Plates 60-68), some sober, some light-hearted, appeared throughout the century, and persist today. It was the revised cult of the Dutch garden a century or more ago that brought the larger-than-life birds and beasts to the shrubs and hedges of our gardens.

The 19th-century interest in historical and formal gardens resulted in the development in the early 1890s of a new school of gardening based on a 'scholarly' approach. William Morris thought most attempts at reconstitution were unlikely to be accurate, but all periods and countries were deemed worthy of study. A famous version from the distant past was the inclusion at Friar Park (Plate 69) of eight 'medieval' gardens based on 15th-century pictures. Reproductions of them in a guide book enabled visitors to compare the documentary evidence with the reconstructions. In the same mode but without a genuine original, the Shakespeare garden at Stratford upon Avon (Plate 70), made some years later, was composed of plants mentioned in the plays. An authentic old garden, that had been swept away in the 18th century, was re-created at Blenheim (Plate 71).

The phrase 'Formal Garden' became current after 1892 on the publication of Sir Reginald Blomfield's *The Formal Garden in England*. By-passing the fashionable natural garden, he advocated the virtues to be found in a return to the formal style. It is perhaps not surprising that this was more popular with architects, who came to be known for their ability and flexibility in handling a variety of garden modes (Plates 72, 73, 74, 75). Long canals and large basins of water, as at Brockenhurst (Plate 77) and Sedgwick Park (Plate 78), were particular features of formal gardens; sometimes they were enclosed by clipped hedges. The formal treatment of water in the garden was in marked contrast to the irregular ponds and small lakes, conveniently provided with punts (Plates 79, 80), that were such features of the English garden.

Edwin Lutyens and Thomas Mawson also tended to favour a certain formality in their gardens. Lutyens' designs benefitted enormously from his association with Gertrude Jekyll (1843-1932), an expert gardener/artist who maintained that 'to plant well needs an *artist* of no mean capacity'. Jekyll, a professionally-trained artist herself, taught that a colour could not stand alone and existed only in relation to other colours. In her many books, including *Colour in the Flower Garden* (1908), she urged gardeners to allow for plenty of green in the garden as a contrast and to arrange flowers blooming at the same time of year close to each other. While not condemning mixed planting (Plates 81, 82, 83), dearly beloved of the Victorians and Edwardians, she detested stupid and ignorant mixtures. Her plantings at Hestercombe about 1906 brought together for the first time her talent and Lutyens' vision of a classical garden on a grand scale. The result is perhaps the finest of their collaborations, incorporating in a happy compromise elements from both natural and formal garden design.

Perhaps just such a spirit of compromise is apparent in the terraces and rose gardens at Madresfield Court (Plate 84), laid out by Thomas Mawson in 1903. Mawson, now rather neglected as a garden architect, was one of the most prolific and widely patronized of his time; his work was particularly admired in Europe. He, like Lutyens, included magnificent pergolas in his schemes. The pergola (Plates 85-94) was a feature imported from Italy, deriving in part from the ancient bower walk. It could be used for the training of fruit trees, as at Gatton Park (Plate 86); but its revival was largely encouraged by an increasing popularity of 'the outdoors'. Queen Victoria enjoyed the shade of a pergola at Osborne (Plate 6). Mawson designed at least three for the various homes of W.H. Lever (later Lord Leverhulme), of which the best is at The Hill, Hampstead (Plates 88-90). A less well-known but impressive pergola was part of the garden scheme designed by Oliver Hill for the Victorian house Moor Close, Berkshire (Plates 91-93), and completed just before the First

World War. Set on a terrace between two pavilions above a sweeping double staircase, this effective little product of the Later Formal Garden Movement was enhanced by wisteria and Jekyll-like plantings nearby.

At Roynton Cottage, Rivington (Plate 94), overlooking the Cheshire Dales, a sturdy pergola was placed by Mawson over a magnificent rockery. The use of rocks in the English garden was not itself new. Ever since the Renaissance, rocks and stone had been used in cascades of water, as at Bowood (Plate 95), to refresh and divert the wanderer weary from long garden trails; but the rockery, as an aesthetic and horticulturally essential setting for alpine and other plants, was a feature which only became popular when the early Victorians took to visiting Switzerland. An enthusiasm for alpine plants developed and the rockery became an increasingly common feature of British gardens. William Robinson took great delight in alpine plants and was influential in spreading their popularity. Some of the best rockeries and rock gardens were constructed about 1900 at, for example Rivington in Cheshire (Plate 94), Gatton Park in Surrey (Plate 100) and Swaylands in Kent (Plates 96, 97). One unique rockery at Friar Park (Plate 98) fancifully rivalled in miniature one of the most famous landscapes in Switzerland; other rock gardens suggested moist dells (Plate 99) or conjured mountain paths.

Rocks are one element of the Japanese garden (Plates 101-104), a type which found great favour at the end of the 19th century and for the next twenty or thirty years. The initial popularity of the form was part of a general *fin-de-siècle* interest in the arts of Japan as they became better known in the West; some of its fame came from appreciative reports by an increasing number of intrepid travellers to the Far East, amongst whom were Britons who, in breaks from upholding the Empire, had ventured from

India or Indonesia into Japan. A few Britons like Mrs Harriet Taylour even lived in Japan, making the most detailed observations of real Japanese gardens, absorbing their spirit and then creating new ones in their proper surroundings. In contrast, most Japanese gardens in England looked distinctly odd. Very few Europeans seem properly to have understood the intentions of a true Japanese garden. Gertrude Jekyll always refused to design one, believing that to do it at all required an expertise that most English gardeners lacked. A proper Japanese garden 'must seem no less than Nature at its best'; its formation is 'an art which has for its conscious or unconscious aim the refreshment of the body by raising the mind to another plane of feeling'. Such subtleties were not really present in the 'Japanese' gardens at Lowther or Friar Park; rather these were fantasy gardens composed of stock Japanese motifs. Nonetheless, some people found such exoticism enormously appealing. As a variant, the garden at Halton House made reference to the sensitivities of Nature but at the same time included Rustic and Gardenesque features. That at Hinchingbrooke, with qualities deriving from its owner's experience of Japan, properly suggested a cool glade.

Among the many types of garden illustrated here, only the Japanese garden, and the rockery with Alpine plants were new to England during the Victorian and Edwardian periods, from which period these photographs largely date. Traces of Japanese influence are apparent in some modern landscaping schemes and there may yet be a revival of the more complex Japanese modes in chic gardens; but the sophisticated Japanese garden has remained a rare exotic. In contrast, the rock garden, more adaptable, and less obviously foreign, became widely established between the wars, and is now, although often a pale suburban shadow of its original glory, ubiquitous.

  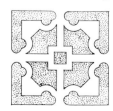  

1 HATFIELD HOUSE, HATFIELD, HERTFORDSHIRE
The garden at Hatfield House, seat of the Salisbury family,
was originally laid out by John Tradescant and Montague
Jennings. An avenue of yew trees, which still survive, was
planted in the Vineyard, probably in the early 18th century.
The Vineyard was first laid out in 1610 by Robert Cecil,
1st Earl of Salisbury. Newton, *c.*1899.

2 (*overleaf*) The East Garden and Maze belong to the early
Victorian age, the maze having been planted in 1841. The
planting of the flower beds had assumed the form illustrated here by 1874, but almost certainly dates back to the
1840s. The beds are in two patterns incorporating the
letters B (for Burghley) and S (for Salisbury). This system
of planting has been replaced with a greatly simplified
arrangement. Neither the Vineyard nor the Maze are open
to the public. Newton, *c.*1899.

3 (*opposite, below*) CHISWICK HOUSE,
HOUNSLOW, GREATER LONDON
Chiswick House was built *c*.1730 for the famous
Palladian architect and connoisseur Lord
Burlington. Lord Burlington's great collection of
ancient statuary was partly housed there, but
much of it was disposed with painstaking
calculation around the garden. Busts representing
the Caesars flank the pleached alley leading to
the East front of the house. In the mid-19th
century this consciously Italian arrangement
found renewed popularity. Newton *c*.1898.

4 GRIMSTON PARK, GRIMSTON, NORTH YORKSHIRE
Grimston Park was rebuilt in 1840 by Decimus Burton for the second Lord Howden
and his wife, Princess Catherine Bagration of Russia. The gardens were laid out by
W.A. Nesfield in the formal Italian style. One feature of these gardens was the
Emperor's Walk, where busts of Roman emperors and sentinel-like yews guarded
the path to the shrine containing a colossal bust of Napoleon. In later years this
noble spot was used as a stand for pheasant shooting, and a loader was once heard
to mark a bird with the exclamation 'There's a cock down back of Calligila!' [sic].
The statuary at Grimston was sold in the 1960s and Nesfield's scheme is rapidly
returning to the wild. Photographer unknown, *c*.1900.

5, 6 (*below and overleaf*) OSBORNE HOUSE, COWES, ISLE OF WIGHT
Osborne House was built between 1847 and 1853 for Queen Victoria and the Prince Consort. Prince Albert
collaborated with Thomas Cubitt on the Italianate design of the house and terraces and he supervised and took
part in the planting of the grounds. Fountains (designed by Gruner and John Bell) and sea allegories (by Theed)
adorned the terraces, as did many small beds of summer flowers. A pergola was included in the scheme.
Newton *c*.1892.

7 WITLEY COURT, GREAT WITLEY, HEREFORD AND WORCESTER
The terraces and garden at Witley Court were laid out in the 1850s by W.A. Nesfield for Lord Ward, later the first Earl of Dudley. This scheme which was extremely costly, included the Perseus fountain (*centre of photograph*), which sent a jet of water thirty metres into the air. William Robinson criticized what he considered was the excess of stone at Witley. Witley Court was gutted by fire in 1937, and is now preserved as a romantic ruin in the guardianship of the Department of the Environment.
Bedford Lemere, *c*.1920.

8 HOLLAND HOUSE, KENSINGTON AND CHELSEA, LONDON
This garden has been known at different stages as the Italian and as the Dutch garden. Formality is the keynote. Some of the first dahlias grown in England outside Kew are said to have been planted here by the third Lady Holland in the early 19th century. Photographer unknown, *c*.1900.

9 BROME HALL, BROME, SUFFOLK
The garden at Brome Hall extending to ten acres, was laid out for Sir E. Clarence Kerrison, who played a large part in its design and developed it from 1823 until his death in 1886. Ornate terraces were laid out near the house. Groups of putti, enveloped in ivy and noisette and tea roses, punctuate the terrace walls. Brome Hall was demolished in 1963. Newton, *c*.1900. Copyright Major D. Hill-Wood.

10 (*opposite*) **HARDWICK HOUSE, WHITCHURCH, OXFORDSHIRE**
Hardwick House was the home of Sir Charles Rose, Bt. a cousin of Henry James. James often stayed here and used the house as a model for Gardencourt in *The Portrait of a Lady* (first published in 1881). This view from the first terrace shows an Italian fountain basin with a lion's head spout, stone seats in the Italian style, and some young topiary bushes. A photograph of Hardwick House was used as the frontispiece for the revised edition of James' masterpiece. Newton, *c*.1910.

11 (*opposite, above*) SOMERLEYTON HALL, SOMERLEYTON, SUFFOLK

Between 1846 and 1851, Somerleyton Hall was transformed by John Thomas, a sculptor who worked for Sir Charles Barry on the Houses of Parliament, but was chosen as architect by Sir Morton Peto for the house he had bought. Having made a fortune building a number of new railways, Peto spared nothing in the aggrandizement of his house and garden. The leading Victorian garden designer William Andrews Nesfield was employed to create the handsome terrace with its *parterre en broderie*, on the west side of the house. The parterre was cut in box and infilled with a groundwork of glittering white stone chippings. The central motif was based upon the old church hinge. Sixteen specimens of Irish yew bordered the terrace. Sir Morton Peto went bankrupt in 1866, but mounting debts had already forced him to sell Somerleyton Hall in 1861. The parterre was maintained by the Crossley family until the Second World War, when it was covered over to prevent the white stone chippings becoming a guide to invading aircraft. After the war, a much simpler arrangement of rosebeds replaced the parterre. Newton, *c*.1898.

12 (*opposite, below*) THORESBY HALL, PERLETHORPE CUM BUDBY, NOTTINGHAMSHIRE

Thoresby Hall was rebuilt in 1865-75, for the third Earl Manvers, by Anthony Salvin. Salvin's nephew, W.A. Nesfield, was responsible for the layout of the garden, which was in fact begun before the house. Many municipal parks are attempts to emulate the gardening style exemplified at Thoresby Hall. Photographer unknown, *c*.1880.

13 (*below*) BLICKLING HALL, BLICKLING, NORFOLK

W.A. Nesfield laid out this scheme for the ninth Marquis and Marchioness of Lothian in 1872. The terrace steps and walls over the excavated site were by Sir Digby Wyatt. This was a very complex scheme with topiary (including some hedges known as the grand pianos), sculpture (originally ornamenting Oxnead Hall in Norfolk, before its break-up in 1809) and carpet-bedding. Lavish colour effects were sought. Later, emphasis was put on roses, pinks, carnations, lilies and other bulbs. In winter, evergreen shrubs were planted. In the 1930s Norah Lindsay, the celebrated plantswoman, devised a simplified scheme here. Photographer unknown, *c*.1895.

14 (*overleaf*) LONGFORD CASTLE, ODSTOCK, WILTSHIRE

The garden at Longford was laid out *c*.1870 for the Earl of Radnor. The Italianate style was chosen at a point when the cult of the Natural Garden was claiming wider public application. In the 1890s, pansies and old-fashioned flowers were planted in the geometrical beds. Two mixed borders, one hundred feet long and full of hardy flowers, were also developed at this time. Newton, *c*.1895.

15 (*opposite, above*) BELTON HOUSE, BELTON AND MANTHORPE, LINCOLNSHIRE
Around 1880, Lord Brownlow partly restored the gardens of his home to roughly their original 17th-century layout. Nonetheless, most of the garden was developed in the grand 19th-century Italian manner. One plant used at Belton was the pansy; the tufted varieties closer in growth, and less unruly, were cultivated in great number. The garden was considered to be at its best in spring. Photographer unknown, *c*.1900.

16 (*opposite, below*) A 'Rosary' was planted inside a circular parterre and along the path leading off from this were herbaceous borders. Basket beds were arranged in the lawn. Photographer unknown, *c*.1900.

17 (*above*) BROME HALL, BROME, SUFFOLK

This parterre was laid out on one of the terraces. Patches of turf were a softening feature in a scheme that included geometrically shaped beds edged in box, and inlaid with broken tiles and stones introducing further colour, mostly blue, grey and white. This system was once much in vogue in England and France. Perfectly trimmed yews and the usual carpet-bedding mixtures enhanced the ensemble. Newton, *c*.1900. Copyright Major D. Hill-Wood.

18 (*opposite, above*) WYNYARD PARK, GRINDON, CLEVELAND
Wynyard Park was built between 1822 and 1841, and has always belonged to the Londonderry family. Extensive flower beds adorned the garden, including this heady display of dahlias and geraniums. Herbaceous plants and other summer bedding, including tropicals, filled the scheme. Garden theorists and horticulturalists, like Loudon and Hibberd, would have taken pleasure in viewing these flowers. Newton, *c*.1895.

19 (*opposite, below*) STANMORE PARK, HARROW, GREATER LONDON
Many beds, massed with nasturtiums, surround a sundial in the garden at Stanmore Park, originally a seat of the Drummonds, a banking family. Photographer unknown, *c*.1900. Copyright G.C. Royle.

20 (*above*) CHEVENING HOUSE, CHEVENING, KENT
The Italian gardens were laid out to the design of the fourth Earl Stanhope, a cousin of Sir Joseph Banks, the first Director of Kew Gardens. Diamond and circular beds, lavishly planted with santolina, annuals, topiary and palms were maintained for nearly one hundred and fifty years. Recently the parterres on the south front of Chevening have been grassed over and the yew trees removed. The west parterre, revised in 1856, remains with new labour-saving plantings. Chevening is presently an official country residence of the Foreign Secretary. Newton, *c*.1920.

21 (*opposite, above*) HUTTON HALL, HUTTON, LANCASHIRE
In this photograph no less than four gardeners are at work. Young plants, newly bedded out, still leave plenty of bare soil requiring regular hoeing. A great variety of types and shapes of flower beds abounds. Standard roses, popular in old-fashioned gardens, line the path. Comfortable garden seats await the inhabitants of Hutton Hall. Photographer unknown, *c.*1890. Copyright M.J. Marson.

22 (*opposite, below*) COMPTON PLACE, EASTBOURNE, EAST SUSSEX
Apart from a walled garden, the flower garden at Compton Place, a seat of the Duke of Devonshire, seems to have been restricted to formal beds hugging the house, which is set in a simple park. Brilliance of display would appear to have been the order of the day when these beds were photographed. Newton, *c.*1916.

23 (*top*) SOMERLEYTON HALL, SOMERLEYTON, SUFFOLK
Splendid herbaceous borders, known to have existed in 1872, flank the central path in the walled kitchen garden at Somerleyton Hall. The kitchen garden is entered through wrought-iron gates set in a massive portico with stone pilasters and coping, decorated on top with two stone urns, each containing a bronze aloe plant. This photograph shows the portico covered with ivy; the urns have since been restored and the ivy cleared away. The herbaceous borders have recently been restored to their original magnificence. The sundial and urns shown in the foreground of this photograph are still in their original positions. Sundials enjoyed a rage at the end of the 19th century, partly because of their old-fashioned associations. J.C. Loudon had had one in his garden many decades before. Newton, *c.*1898.

24 (*centre*) EATON HALL, EATON, CHESHIRE
The photograph shows a herbaceous border. The garden at Eaton Hall was developed in the 19th century for the Dukes of Westminster. Newton, *c.*1900.

25 (*bottom*) MELCHET COURT, MELCHET PARK AND PLAITFORD, HAMPSHIRE
Superbly full herbaceous borders lead to a lodge (or the gardener's house) at Melchet Court, which was built in the 1860s. The main body of the garden was laid out then, although it was further developed in the 1920s. Melchet Court is now an institution. Newton, *c.*1929.

26 (*opposite*) COMPTON HOUSE, COMPTON
BASSETT, WILTSHIRE
Compton House was built in the 18th century
and rebuilt in 1932-5 by George Kennedy. In
1911 the house was a property of the Walker
Heneage family, but was occupied by Lieut. Col.
Alfred Western Hatchell Hornsby-Drake.
Fred Marsh, 1917. Copyright C.R. Fraser-Jenkins.

27 (*top*) SUTTON PLACE, WOKING, SURREY
The largely ruined Sutton Place was restored
c.1877 for Mr Lawrence Harrison. Old walled
gardens survived. In one was an octagonal
garden house belonging to the earliest period of
garden work at Sutton. Fruit trees and vegetables
were planted behind beds filled with snap-
dragons, penstemons, phlox, *Coreopsis*, monks-
hoods, tiger lilies, *Achillea* and golden rod. Dwarf
Nepeta and *Sedum superba* edged the path.
Ancient apple trees provided shade.
    One of the walled gardens was later converted
by Lady Northcliffe into a sunken garden,
another into a Japanese garden. Sutton Place is
currently being re-landscaped to the design of
Sir Geoffrey Jellicoe. Newton, *c*.1914.

28 (*centre*) AQUALATE HALL, FORTON,
STAFFORDSHIRE
John Nash built Aqualate Hall *c*.1808 for Sir
John Boughey, Bt. Humphry Repton may have
created the ornamental garden, but this may
have been developed in the mid-19th century.
The scheme with its serpentine path, conifers,
yews, and endless plots of bedding plants was
entirely Gardenesque in character and was still
intact in the 1920s when the Hall, partly ruined
by fire in 1910, was rebuilt. Bedford Lemere,
1892.

29 (*bottom*) SAND HUTTON HALL,
SAND HUTTON, NORTH YORKSHIRE
Small flower beds dot the lawn beside a path
that winds by a thatched gazebo. This Gardenesque area may have been laid out about the
time that the house, built by Carr, was re-
modelled by Salvin in 1839-41. Sand Hutton was
the seat of the Walker family. W.J. Day, *c*.1907.

30 AVONBANK, STRATFORD UPON AVON, WARWICKSHIRE
In the late 19th century Avonbank belonged to a Mrs Flower. The terrace and garden of this upper middle-class villa have all the qualities of privacy and nature unconfined that were lacking in the hugh Italianate schemes laid out for great houses. Newton, *c*.1900.

31 MEXBOROUGH, SOUTH YORKSHIRE
Ideal cottage life – everlasting pea round the door, nasturtiums lining the path. The photographer may well have found this old cottager reading in the sunshine, but it should be remembered that contemporary photographers like Gertrude Jekyll or Henry Taunt were given to stage-managing the willing or hapless inhabitants of the place into arty or imaginative poses. W.J. Day, *c*.1905.

32 (*opposite, above*) GREAT TANGLEY MANOR, WONERSH, SURREY
Great Tangley was the seat of Mr Wickham Flower who commissioned Philip Webb to restore and extend the old manor house between 1886 and 1897. Under the guidance of Mr Whiteman, the garden and landscape specialist, the gardens were laid out in 1884 on an old farmyard site where no ornamental gardens had previously existed. The work called for eighteen labourers at a time over a period of six months. In this photograph, roses grow informally and abundantly near, and over, the house in the best cottage garden spirit. W.J. Day, *c*.1900.

33 (*opposite, below*) EASTON NESTON, EASTON NESTON, NORTHAMPTONSHIRE
One necessity at great houses was a highly organized and productive kitchen garden providing vegetables and cut flowers for the benefit of large families, their many servants and frequent houseparties. The compartmentalized and straight-forward arrangement of kitchen gardens was not without influence on the Robinsonian and Old-Fashioned Garden. Most kitchen gardens have now had to be grassed over or converted to other uses. Photographer unknown, *c*.1880.

34 (*opposite*) ALTHORP HOUSE, ALTHORP, NORTHAMPTONSHIRE
In 1901, Silas Cole, head gardener at Althorp House to the 5th Earl Spencer, developed a new strain of sweet pea, large and with frilly petals, of which the shell-pink 'Countess Spencer' was the first. This development ensured the popularity of the sweet pea as a garden and show flower. Newton, *c*.1903.

35 (*above*) GARNONS, MANSELL GAMAGE, HEREFORD AND WORCESTER
The garden and park at Garnons, seat of the Cotterell family, are thought to have been modified at the end of the 18th century by Humphry Repton, the first person to adopt the term 'landscape gardening'. Repton reintroduced flower beds, but the scheme in this photograph is of a much later date. Ribbon borders such as these were common features of Victorian gardens, but the great 19th- and early 20th-century horticultural theorist and critic, William Robinson, held acerbic views as to their merit. Photographer unknown, *c*.1870. Copyright Sir John Cotterell, Bt.

36 (*overleaf*) GUNNERSBURY PARK, HOUNSLOW, GREATER LONDON
Lord Rothschild owned Gunnersbury Park, the garden of which was merged with that of Gunnersbury House, the home of Mr Lionel de Rothschild. Both men were connoisseurs of rare and beautiful plants, and enjoyed creating a garden filled with choice specimens.
  Basket beds were popular in the 19th century. Here geraniums and other flowers are gathered under iron handles dressed by rambling blooms. Newton, *c*.1900.

37 CLAREMONT, ESHER, SURREY
Banks of penstemons planted in ribbon form, fill this border at Claremont, which was at this time the home of the widowed Duchess of Albany, daughter-in-law of Queen Victoria. After the war ended in 1918, Claremont was let to a girls' school, Leatherhead Court. Newton, *c.*1917.

38 GUNNERSBURY PARK, HOUNSLOW, GREATER LONDON
An alcove on the terraced filled with exotics. Newton, *c.*1900.

39 (*opposite*) **COBHAM HALL, COBHAM, KENT**
Rhododendrons in full bloom grace the lake in the park at Cobham Hall, which was originally landscaped by Humphry Repton around 1790. The genus *Rhododendron* is exceptionally large; the introduction of many Asiastic Species in the 19th and 20th centuries and successful hybridization have given them an important place in British gardens. Cobham Hall was the seat of the Earls of Darnley, but is now a girls' boarding school. Newton, *c.*1900.

40 (*top*) DEEPDENE, DORKING, SURREY
Deepdene was rebuilt by Thomas Hope in 1843.
At the same time the grounds were extended.
Masses and banks of rhododendrons and
conifers were planted, often intercepted by
winding paths. In striking contrast to the
rhododendrons is this *Araucaria* or Pacific
conifer, more commonly known as the monkey
puzzle tree. The species was introduced to
Britain in 1795 and was widely planted from
1840 onwards. These trees, now in their
maturity, are a conspicuous feature in the
grounds of many Victorian country houses.
Newton, *c*.1899.

41 (*centre*) HINTON ADMIRAL, BRANSGORE,
HAMPSHIRE
Hinton Admiral was the home of Sir George
Meyrick, Bt. who took a great pride in improving
and cultivating his garden, which included a big
rock garden and a terrace laid out by the
architect Harold Peto. One of the many features
of the extensive gardens, through which thirty
peacocks were allowed to wander at will, was
this pampas walk. Pampas grass was introduced
in England in 1848, but was more widely and
successfully grown from the 1860s onwards.
W.J. Day, *c*.1910.

42 (*bottom*) CLANDON PARK, WEST
CLANDON, SURREY
An exotic effect is achieved from this planting of
an isolated clump of New Zealand tree ferns.
Clandon Park was the home of the Onslow
family. Newton, date unknown.

43 (*opposite*) BULSTRODE PARK, GERRARDS
CROSS, BUCKINGHAMSHIRE
This planting of young rhododendrons gives
little hint of the dense growth they will make in
their maturity.
Bulstrode Park was rebuilt for Sir John
Ramsden, Bt. in 1870. Newton, *c*.1904.

44 (*overleaf, top*) ABBEY GARDENS,
TRESCO, SCILLY ISLES
Augustus Smith began these gardens in the
1830s. As the island was virtually tree-less an
immense sixty-acre windbreak of huge flat-
topped Monterey pines and macrocarpas was
planted. Over two hundred men were required
to plant them and carve out the terraces for the
garden, in which were compressed over four
thousand species drawn from the five continents.
Smith's family have continued to develop Abbey
Gardens over a period of one hundred and fifty
years. Photographer unknown, *c*.1900.

45 *(below)* CRAGSIDE, CARTINGTON, NORTHUMBERLAND
The natural terrain of Cragside was a wilderness of barren rock, scrub and heather. This was transformed for Lord Armstrong into a vast pleasure ground on which seven million trees and innumerable rhododendrons and azaleas were planted between 1870 and 1883. Some of the rock was left visible. This entirely artificial but very romantic forest made a perfect setting for the *schloss* perched on a crag. Cragside, which was designed by Richard Norman Shaw, is now owned by the National Trust.
Bedford Lemere, 1891.

46 *(opposite)* PYRFORD COURT, WOKING, SURREY
Giant lilies (*Cardiocrinum*) were planted in clumps in the wood at Pyrford Court, where they appear to have thrived. The species was introduced to England in the 19th century.
Newton, *c.*1920.

47, 48 (*opposite*) HINCHINGBROOKE, HUNTINGDON AND GODMANCHESTER, CAMBRIDGESHIRE
Hinchingbrooke belonged to the Earl of Sandwich who developed gardens there towards the end of the 19th century. This garden shows many of the characteristics of the Queen Anne or Old-Fashioned Garden, although new plants were mixed with old. At the same time, traces of the Italian style are evident. Newton, *c.*1907.

49 (*above*) DITTON PARK, DATCHET, BERKSHIRE
Ditton Park, which became the seat of Lord Wolverton, was built in 1813-17. In the much later arrangement of this walled garden, the principal elements are bush and standard roses. In the second half of the 19th century, enthusiasm for the rose was matched by the remarkable pace of developments in the breeding of new varieties, particularly in France and Britain. Newton, *c.*1899.

50 (*opposite*) OLD FORGE, QUALITY STREET, MERSTHAM, SURREY

The straight hedges and borders and canes of a raspberry bed, contrived but self-effacing, were typical features of the old-fashioned garden. The rustic wood furniture shown here accords with 18th-century precedents. But William Robinson expressed distaste for wood furniture outside, not least for the reason that rot quickly set in.

Quality Street was an early 18th-century street that was extended at the end of the 19th century. The actors Ellaline Terriss and Seymour Hicks were living at the Old Forge at the time that they were appearing in Barrie's *Quality Street*; hence the name of the street. Newton, *c*.1905.

51 (*top*) CLAREMONT PARK, ESHER, SURREY

This part of the garden at Claremont exemplifies the late 19th-century taste for prettiness. The garland of roses around the pool corresponds with contemporary trends in book illustration and interior decoration.

The arrangement of the garden no doubt reflected the taste of the Duke and Duchess of Albany. The Duke, who brought his bride here in 1882, took a lively interest in artistic matters. His daughter Princess Alice, Countess of Athlone, became an indefatigable gardener at Brantridge Park, creating a large rock garden there. Newton, *c*.1917.

52 (*centre*) LITTLEHOME, GUILDOWN ROAD, GUILDFORD, SURREY

Littlehome was built by C.F.A. Voysey for G. Müntzer in 1906-7. The character of the garden was partly determined by the sloping site, but Dutch/Old-Fashioned garden motifs are also apparent long after the first popularity of the movement. Photographer unknown, *c*.1909. Copyright RIBA.

PYRFORD COURT, WOKING, SURREY

Pyrford Court was begun in 1906 for Lord Iveagh. The scheme included various individual gardens. One was laid out in the Dutch manner, with brick walls, straight paths, lawn and traditional flowers.

53 (*bottom*) Peony Walk. Newton, *c*.1924.

54 (*overleaf*) Standard roses in the Dutch garden. Newton, *c*.1924.

55 CORNBURY PARK, CORNBURY, OXFORDSHIRE

This chestnut avenue, reminiscent of those at Windsor or Hampton Court, was planted by the second Lord Churchill and his wife, Jane, who was a friend and Lady-in-Waiting to Queen Victoria. The avenue was a happy addition to the important and little known 17th-century landscape upon which John Evelyn had originally advised the Earl of Clarendon. The Duke and Duchess of Albany planted a similar chestnut avenue at Claremont in 1882. H.W. Taunt, c.1895. Copyright Oxfordshire County Libraries.

56 BYRAM HALL, BYRAM CUM SUTTON, NORTH YORKSHIRE

The hornbeam avenue on the north terrace at Byram Hall was planted in 1873. Byram Hall was the seat of the Ramsdens. W.J. Day, c.1900.

57 (*opposite, above*) REDLEAF, PENSHURST, KENT

The grounds at Redleaf were laid out early in the 19th century by William Wells. This drive bordered by conifers and rhododendrons is almost certainly of a much later date. Bedford Lemere, 1894.

58 (*opposite, below*) LEVENS HALL, LEVENS, CUMBRIA

The celebrated topiary garden at Levens was laid out for James Graham by Monsieur Beaumont, the French gardener, around 1700. The garden, reviled by William Robinson, is now however much visited by the general public. Newton, *c.*1899.

59 (*top*) ELVASTON CASTLE, ELVASTON, DERBYSHIRE

The grounds at Elvaston Castle were laid out between 1830 and 1850 by William Barron (from the Botanic Gardens in Edinburgh) for the Earl of Harrington. The Alhambra Garden, illustrated here, was just one feature of these famous gardens, renowned for their wide selection of species trees and topiary. The site was originally rejected by Capability Brown 'because the place is so flat, and there is a want of capability in it'. At one time a staff of eighty gardeners worked on this estate. The gardens were restored in 1968-70 and are open to the public. London, Midland and Scottish Railway Company, 1908.

60 (*centre*) ALDERMASTON COURT, ALDERMASTON, BERKSHIRE

Aldermaston Court was built *c.*1851 for Daniel Burr by the architect Philip Charles Hardwick. It was bought in 1893 by Charles Keyser, a grandson of the architect Edward Blore. Mr Keyser also owned Warren House, Stanmore.

Fantastic cones of yew line a path to the terrace, a feature that provided a setting for one episode in the BBC televised dramatization of the life of Nancy Astor. Aldermaston Court is now a property of the Ministry of Defence. Newton, *c.*1899.

61 (*bottom*) THORNBURY CASTLE, THORNBURY, AVON

Thornbury Castle, begun in 1508, was restored by the architect Salvin in 1854. It is probable that it was at this time that the whimsical castellated yew hedges were planted. The experience of passing between these hedges can only have added a new dimension to Thornbury's age-old fame as a 'Goodly Gardeyn to Walk Ynn'.

In 1907 Thornbury was the seat of Mr Edward Stafford Howard. Newton, *c.*1907.

62 (*opposite, above*) MELCHET COURT,
MELCHET PARK AND PLAITFORD,
HAMPSHIRE
This row of sentry boxes at Melchet Court
guards an ancient pine. Newton, *c*.1929.

63 (*opposite, below*) MADRESFIELD COURT,
MADRESFIELD, HEREFORD AND
WORCESTER
A large arena used as a bowling green was
framed by a clipped hedge in whose niches were
placed busts of the Caesers. William Robinson
dismissed topiary because of its Italian origins,
but Gertrude Jekyll, who had visited Italy in her
youth, was more appreciative. Newton, *c*.1907.

64 (*right*) BROME HALL, BROME, SUFFOLK
Topiary arches are in juxtaposition with obelisks
and globes at the far side of the garden at Brome.
Newton, *c*.1900. Copyright Major D. Hill-Wood.

65 (*below*) WARREN HOUSE, STANMORE,
HARROW, GREATER LONDON
The Dutch influence is evident in this topiary
garden at Warren House. Newton, *c*.1910.

66 (*top*) STONE HALL, LITTLE EASTON, ESSEX
Topiary sundials such as this at Stone Hall, a
smaller house on the Easton Lodge Estate,
enjoyed a vogue in Edwardian gardens. A larger
topiary sundial was a feature of the garden at
Broughton Castle. Easton Lodge was inherited
by Daisy, Countess of Warwick. Newton, *c*.1907.

67 (*centre*) BROUGHTON CASTLE,
BROUGHTON, OXFORDSHIRE
Broughton Castle was rented by Lord and Lady
Gordon-Lennox towards the end of the 19th
century. A desolate garden was transformed
with the help of four gardeners and a boy. One
new feature was a fanciful reproduction of a
medieval herb garden, with the plants at lawn
level for treading upon, thus releasing the aroma.
The entrance was heralded by letters in clipped
santolina, 'Ye Herbe Garden'. Herb clipping,
forming texts and decorative patterns, is a
traditional practice. Newton, *c*.1898.

68 (*bottom*) NUNEHAM PARK, NUNEHAM
COUNTNEY, OXFORDSHIRE
The coronet and cypher of Lord Harcourt was
the theme of this topiary garden outside the
entrance of Nuneham Park, the setting of many
brilliant Edwardian house parties.
Newton, *c*.1918.

69 (*above, right*) FRIAR PARK, HENLEY,
OXFORDSHIRE
Friar Park was built in 1896 for Sir Frank Crisp,
who collaborated with his architect Mr M. Clarke
Edwards. Some of the gardens were based on
15th-century pictures. These included the
Elizabethan Herb Garden and the Garden of
Sweet Smells and Savours. This photograph
shows the Grey Garden with the Blue Garden in
the background. Similarities and dissimilarities
between ancient gardens and Old-Fashioned or
even Robinsonian gardens are apparent. Lady
Ottoline Morrell may have been influenced by
these gardens when she created the parterre at
Garsington Manor. Newton, *c*.1903.

70 (*right*) SHAKESPEARE'S GARDEN, NEW
PLACE, STRATFORD UPON AVON,
WARWICKSHIRE
The garden at New Place, laid out in 1919-21 by
Ernest Law for the Birthplace Trust, was filled
with plants mentioned in Shakespeare's plays,
such as box, savory, cotton lavender, thyme, and
other herbs and flowers. A palisaded garden
within it, which is divided up into squares, is
known as the Elizabethan Garden.
Newton, *c*.1924.

71 (*overleaf*) BLENHEIM PALACE, BLENHEIM,
OXFORDSHIRE
The original parterre outside the east front of
Blenheim Palace had been swept away in the
late 18th century by Capability Brown. At the
end of the 19th century, a parterre roughly on
the lines of the original, was laid out. It still has
the distinctively Victorian arrangement of
bedding plants. Spiky aloes shoot out of vases on
the steps. Three gardeners are busy in this scene.
H.W. Taunt, *c*.1893. Copyright Oxfordshire
County Libraries.

72 (*opposite, above*) DOWNSIDE, LEATHERHEAD, SURREY
Downside was built in about 1860 for William Lee and was subsequently bought by Alfred Tate about 1888. He eventually altered the house, emphasizing its Italianate aspect. On one side of the garden he created extensive rose gardens (he was an exhibitor at all the great rose shows). This succession of terraces in a formal Dutch/Italianate style had not been made when Downside was featured in *Country Life* in 1898 and probably belongs to the first decade of the 20th century. Newton, *c*.1910.

73 (*opposite, below*) COOMBE COURT, KINGSTON UPON THAMES, GREATER LONDON
Coombe Court (built in 1869 as Coombe Warren) was the childhood home of John Galsworthy. His father sold it in 1875 to Daniel Watney, who later sold it to the Earl and Countess de Grey, later the second Marquis and Marchioness of Ripon, who made extensive alterations and enlargements. These changes included a transformation of the garden from a simple area, planted at intervals with conifers, into a grand Italian garden.

Lavish and ultra-fashionable houseparties were given by the de Greys, who were often the hosts of King Edward VII and Queen Alexandra. Dame Nellie Melba sang here.

Coombe Court was demolished in 1931 – and the garden has subsequently been built over. Newton, *c*.1913.

74 (*above*) PYRFORD COURT, WOKING, SURREY
The Italian garden at Pyrford Court, built just before the First World War, was enclosed by a yew hedge, and paved in brick, which was laid in a herringbone pattern. Small square lily pools abounded, strategically placed between rectangular flowerbeds, which were filled with summer plants. Terracotta and stone urns further evoked the Continent as did the barrels filled with agapanthus. Newton, *c*.1920.

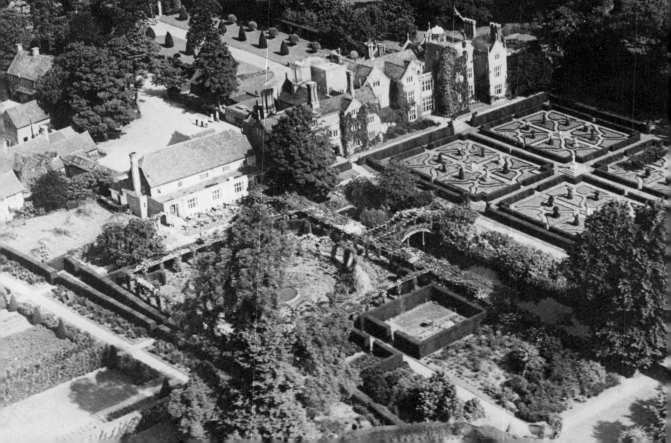

75 (*opposite, above*) MOOR CLOSE, BINFIELD, BERKSHIRE

The intricate system of crossing vistas in the garden at Moor Close was contrived by the architect Oliver Hill. A succession of steps and terraces led to a sunken lily pool. Newton. *c*.1920.

76 (*opposite, below*) GREAT FOSTERS, EGHAM, SURREY

These gardens were completed for the Hon. Gerald Montague just after the First World War. Parterres near the house, containing 'Old English' flowers, contrasted with informal plantings of shrubs and flowers within a frame of simple hedges. A circular rose garden and a pergola were laid out near the old moat, which was crossed by a Chinese bridge. Great Fosters is now a hotel. Photographer unknown, *c*.1922.

77 (*top*) BROCKENHURST PARK, BROCKENHURST, HAMPSHIRE

This formal garden with its canal was laid out for Mr John Morant early in the 20th century. The emphasis was on green sculpture and forms rather than flowers. Orange trees in tubs and topiary bushes and hedges frame this long water, the whole being redolent of Italian gardens.

   The house has been rebuilt but the canal and hedges remain. W.J. Day, *c*.1906.

78 (*centre*) SEDGWICK PARK, NUTHURST, WEST SUSSEX

Sedgwick Park was the home of a Mrs Henderson, who took delight in a large water garden. Italianate hedges framed a large basin of water on whose calm surface waterlilies floated. An angry fish and a Japanese lamp seem faintly at odds with the whole. W.J. Day, *c*.1909.

79 (*bottom*) CLANDON PARK, WEST CLANDON, SURREY

On a breathless summer day, a punt on the water offered a welcome retreat from the gloom of oppressive country houses, or the less leisurely recreation of tennis. A punt also offered tempting prospects to romantic couples seeking a moment away from family, friends or chaperones. Considerable expertise is required to manage a punt, and many a young country-house guest found himself parting company from punt and pole and meeting the smack of the water. Newton, *c*.1925.

80 (*overleaf*) GRIM'S DYKE, HARROW, GREATER LONDON

Grim's Dyke was built in 1872 by Norman Shaw for the painter Goodall. It was later the home of the famous librettist W.S. Gilbert. A punt house stood by the lake. Gilbert died here in 1911, of heart failure, after plunging into the lake to go to the aid of two lady guests who had got into difficulties. Newton, *c*.1900.

81 (*top*) GATTON PARK, REIGATE, SURREY
This border is a fine example of the new kind of
mixed planting that emerged in the early 20th
century. The softer effects of snow-in-summer
contrast with the spiky leaves and brilliant
blooms of many irises. There is total ground
cover but regular dividing and replanting would
be a necessity.

Gatton Park was purchased in 1888 by
Jeremiah Colman (later chairman of the mustard-
making company), who commissioned the
garden specialist Mr Edward White to develop
the garden. Newton, *c*.1910.

82 (*centre*) RIBSTON HALL, GREAT RIBSTON,
NORTH YORKSHIRE
Ribston Hall was the seat of Major J.W. Dent
when this photograph was taken. The tone of his
garden was quiet, but variety of plants was
permissible. This island bed, graced by a solemn
maiden, is a typical Edwardian example of mixed
planting, with delphiniums, astilbes, lilies and
Canterbury bells in abundance. W.J. Day, *c*.1908.

83 (*bottom*) 12 EMBANKMENT GARDENS,
CHELSEA, LONDON
A town garden is often a formal affair, but the
formality of this small walled garden, with its
stone paving, straight hedges and Italian-inspired
statuary is softened by the free mixture of plants.
Roses and irises mix with *Rudbeckia* and bergenia.
Agapanthus and lilies line a path at the back. The
gate piers and statuary incline at a slightly crazy
angle, adding a note of picturesque decay. Care-
fully planted trees inside and outside the garden
suggest a more rural setting than the actuality.

A Lady Victoria Manners lived at 12 Embankment Gardens during the first twenty years or so
of this century. Newton, *c*.1919.

84 MADRESFIELD COURT, MADRESFIELD, HEREFORD AND WORCESTER

The terrace and rose gardens were laid out by Thomas Mawson in 1903. The plantings, rich in lavenders and santolinas, suggest some sympathy with Gertrude Jekyll's style. However, Mawson's work was characterized by a stricter classicism than that of Jekyll, which drew on the tradition of the cottage gardener and was inspired by an artist's sense of colour. The terrace conceals a moat; beyond a further terrace, clipped yew hedges form a series of three-sided rooms. Madresfield Court was the home of the Lygon family, on whom Evelyn Waugh is thought to have partly based the Marchmain family in *Brideshead Revisited*. Bedford Lemere, 1907.

85 (*opposite*) AMMERDOWN HOUSE, KILMERSDON, SOMERSET
This pretty pergola of larch poles contrasts with the heavier more solid structures that went up in other gardens. It also contrasted with the pergola of concrete pillars made by Lutyens in the same garden, nearer the more formal parterres he laid out in 1901 for Lord Hylton. W.J. Day, *c*.1908.

86 (*above*) GATTON PARK, REIGATE, SURREY
The original function of the pergola had been to support fruit trees and vines. In Victorian and Edwardian gardens such a useful adjunct as this pear alley could also be appreciated for its beauty and for the shade it afforded. Newton, *c*.1910.

87 (*overleaf*) FLIXTON HALL, FLIXTON, NEAR BUNGAY, SUFFOLK
Mrs Allan Adair sits with a book under the scented shade of this wisteria-clad pergola, which is thought to have been commissioned by Sir Frederick Adair about the turn of the century. At Flixton Sir Frederick also laid out an unusual garden of large rocks, conifers and ferns, set in grass.
   Flixton Hall, built by the architect Salvin in 1844-50, was demolished in 1953. S.R. Bennett, *c*.1928.
Copyright Maj.-Gen. Sir Allan Adair, Bt.

THE HILL, HAMPSTEAD, LONDON

This pergola was part of the large 'town garden' scheme created by Thomas Mawson for W.H. Lever in 1906. The long pergola screens off most of the garden. Local residents objected to its construction on the grounds that it disfigured the natural beauty of Hampstead Heath. Mr Lever, who did not wish to be overlooked, rejoiced in garden parties under its shady beams. The pergola, rather gaunt when new, is now romantically clad in a luxuriant growth of climbing plants. The garden is open to the public.

88 (*opposite*) Part of the pergola running opposite the house. *Treillage* was very popular in the Edwardian era. Newton, *c.*1910.

89 (*top*) View from the Belvedere towards the temple. Newton, *c.*1906.

90 (*bottom*) Climbing roses cluster round a column by the steps. Newton, *c.*1910.

MOOR CLOSE, BINFIELD, BERKSHIRE
Moor Close was built in 1881. In 1911, Oliver Hill, in an early commission, altered the house for Mr C. Birch Crisp. Hill also created new gardens, the highlight of which was a pair of pavilions linked by a pergola.

91 (*top*) A horseshoe staircase in stone descends from one terrace to another. Newton, *c.*1920.

92 (*centre*) View beneath the pergola looking towards the interior of one of the pavilions with its circular window. The courtyard to the left is cobbled. Newton, *c.*1920.

93 (*bottom*) Another view from behind the pergola. Moor Close is now Newbold College. The pergola survives, but is in a sad state of decay. Newton, *c.*1920.

94 ROYNTON COTTAGE, RIVINGTON, LANCASHIRE
In 1905 Thomas Mawson built a bungalow retreat for W.H. Lever. Not far from the bungalow (later burnt down by suffragettes), a pergola was placed over a massive rockery. The site, exposed to bracing winds, necessitated a pergola of robust construction. It enjoyed a spectacular view, perched on a one thousand foot contour on the slope of Rivington Pike. W.J. Day, *c.*1910.

95 (*opposite*) BOWOOD, CALNE, WILTSHIRE
The cascade at Bowood, based on a picture by
Gaspard Poussin, was constructed *c.*1785, to the
design of Mr Hamilton of Pains Hill, assisted by
Mr Josiah Lane, and 'finished' by the second Earl
of Shelburne. W.J. Day, *c.*1906.

96 (*top*) SWAYLANDS, PENSHURST, KENT
In 1886, Mr. G. Drummond, with his gardener
Mr Hosier, began to create new gardens in the
park of his home, re-built by the architect Devey
in the second half of the 19th century. The most
magnificent feature to emerge during the next
twenty years was a giant rockery, largely planted
with spring flowers, such as arabis, purple
aubretia, yellow alyssum, many alpine phlox,
and *Gypsophila prostrata*. W.J. Day, *c.*1906.

97 (*centre*) Rocks and ferns are set between
shrubs and trees – a miniature canyon-like effect
is achieved. Until recently, these walks have
been completely overgrown, but they have now
been cleared by the staff and children of
Swaylands School. W.J. Day, *c.*1906.

98 (*bottom*) FRIAR PARK, HENLEY,
OXFORDSHIRE
Sir Frank Crisp's eccentricities were reflected in
his garden. In 1905 Lady Ottoline Morrell visited
Friar Park where she found Crisp, dressed in
frock coat and top hat, proudly showing his
visitors round the garden, which had 'Sham
Swiss mountains and passes decorated by china
chamois'. Twenty-three thousand tons of rock
were used in the construction of this garden
which accommodated an extensive collection of
alpine and other rock garden plants.
Newton, *c.*1907.

99 (*overleaf*) GREAT TANGLEY, WONERSH,
SURREY
This dell-like rock garden with its sheets of
spreading alpine plants was praised by Gertrude
Jekyll, who had known Great Tangley before the
garden was created by Wickham Flower. Rocks
of local Bargate stone were used in the scheme.
Shrubs shut this part of the garden off from the
rest, making it a wonderful discovery. Bedford
Lemere, 1916.

100 (*above*) GATTON PARK, REIGATE, SURREY
This charmingly-planted rock garden was built for Sir Jeremiah Colman around the turn of the 20th century by Messrs Pulham and Sons, one of the firms that pioneered the construction of rock gardens. Newton, *c*.1906.

101 (*opposite, above*) FRIAR PARK, HENLEY, OXFORDSHIRE
This exuberant rendition in the Japanese manner is everything one would expect from what is known of Sir Frank Crisp. After his death in 1919, Friar Park was sold. Many years later it was owned by Beatle George Harrison in whose psychedelic era the toys and jokes of Crisp's imagination found renewed appreciation. Newton, *c*.1907.

102 (*opposite, below*) LOWTHER CASTLE, LOWTHER, CUMBRIA
A Japanese Garden was laid out to the east of Lowther Castle by the fifth Earl of Lonsdale. Rock gardens and a scented garden were nearby.
Lowther Castle, built in 1806, was gutted in 1957 and stands as a romantic ruin. W.J. Day, 1910.

103 (*above*) HINCHINGBROOKE, HUNTINGDON AND GODMANCHESTER, CAMBRIDGESHIRE
This Japanese Garden was laid out for the Earl of Sandwich who had travelled in the Far East, and who had been much impressed with all he saw. A thatched tea-house was placed on an island, while little slopes and valleys, a miniature lake and a stream, completed the frame. Bronze cranes and geese enlivened the scheme. Newton, *c*.1907.

104 (*opposite*) HALTON HOUSE, HALTON, BUCKINGHAMSHIRE
Although described as the Japanese Garden, this scheme in which Rustic and Gardenesque elements are apparent makes a change from the more aggressive essays in the style seen elsewhere. Chopped logs form steps to a thatched gazebo worthy of the 18th or early 19th century. William Robinson would not have approved.
Bedford Lemere, 1892.

INDEX

References in roman numerals refer to introduction pages. Other references refer to the plates.